Are men really everything they're cracked up to be?

Men... they don't come with owner's manuals, so here's the lowdown... *in gruesome detail.*

Men... it turns out you *were* right... *it IS all their fault!*

Men... when they act as if there's a tiny, evil person living in their under shorts, *it just might be true!*

....

"Like the ebola virus, **The Trouble With Men** *will consume you entirely and rock your shivering body with spasms — of laughter!"*

—Edna Gougeman, PhD, *winner of the Bricklestone Prize for Outstanding Germology*

The Trouble With Men © 1996 by Kitty Mancini

For information, or to order copies of this book, contact

Hypertext Publishing Group
P.O. Box 420686
San Diego, CA 92142

Or call toll-free: 1-800-75 HYPER

E-Mail: HPGBooks@AOL.com

The cartoons on pages 17, 19, 35, 39, 47, 83, 110, & 119 are reprinted from *Stand Back, I Think I'm Gonna Laugh*, © 1994 with permission from Laugh Lines Press, and Rina Piccolo.

Book design by John Del Gaizo

Cover design by Dunn & Associates
Cover cartoons by Rina Piccolo

Printed in the United States of America

Library of Congress Catalog Card Number
95-79165

Mancini, Kitty

The Trouble With Men / Kitty Mancini
    p.   c m.

ISBN 0-9648010-9-4

1.Humor-Women's Studies
I. Kitty Mancini 1958-

*To Fred,
Happy reading!
Kitty Mancini
7-96*

*Rina Piccolo
July '96*

The Trouble
With Men

Kitty Mancini

**cartoons by Rina Piccolo
and R.C. Aradio**

Hypertext Publishing Group
New York • Los Angeles

ACKNOWLEDGEMENTS

X-tra special thanks to the following people who's talent,
ideas and creative force have shaped this book:

Ruth Tara, *(who inspired the idea for this book
with her dates from hell stories)*
Rina Piccolo, *(for her brilliantly funny cartoons),*
R.C. Aradio *(ditto on the cartoons),*
J. Del Gaizo *(copy commando & design dandy),*
Darlene Colburn *(for her constant feedback
& witty insights)* and my mother,
Ginny *(for her keen observations
& delightfully warped words of wisdom.)*

A re you searching for an honest man? One who says, "Hi, I'm the guy from hell. Will you go out with me?"

"I'm polite and thoughtful," he adds, "but after we're intimate, I'll belch like a rhino, send flowers only if we have an argument— and after you marry me, my gut will expand and I'll wear sweat suits covered with lint balls for the rest of my life."

If he were honest, you wouldn't waste time thinking you've discovered Superman when he's really Homer Simpson.

My friend, Donna, age 35 and single, whines, "If the President knew about my relationships, he would declare them national disasters."

"Relationships aren't for everyone," I say. "Look at Prince Charles and Princess Di. Donald Trump and Ivana. Liz Taylor and Nicky Hilton, and Michael Wilding, and Eddie Fisher, and Richard Burton...and Richard Burton."

"I want to get married," she says. "I want a baby."

"And if you can't find a suitable husband?"

"I'll get another dog."

She has seventeen dogs and I worry.

"Look at all these women having babies at 50. I still have time," she says, diapering her Chihuahua.

"There's a sperm bank downtown," I suggest. "If your donor is anything like the losers you've dated, at least you won't have to meet him."

Donna looks for love in all the wrong places.

"I know a decent man exists somewhere," Donna says. "Do you think there's life on Saturn?"

"Man hunting is like shopping for a car," I reply. "Decide which types will perform best and recognize which types will be trouble."

Handle your first date like a test drive. If he fits into the following categories, turn off the ignition and shout, "Next!"

MR. TERRITORIAL

It's your first dinner date and you just sat at your table. He's cross-examining you while you're trying to read the menu. He's wringing his hands, asking you the same question over and over.

"So how many guys have you dated?"

"Eight or nine," you foolishly answer.

"Did you have sex with them?" he asks, annoyed.

"No. Never."

"Did you *kiss* any of them?" He's twisting the French bread like it's your ex-boyfriend's neck.

"So you cheated on me," he glares.

Your appetizer hasn't arrived and he hates you already. He despises every guy who's ever touched you—including your dentist. He's jealous of your gynecologist. He knows those pap smears can drive women wild. According to Mr. Territorial, any woman who's not Mother Theresa or Julia Child is definitely a slut.

MAMMA'S BOY

He lives with his parents. His room is eerily clean. His bed is always made. His underwear is ironed and folded into neat little squares. Everywhere the two of you go, his mother is a few paces behind. She pats him on the tushy when she kisses him good-bye.

You always find yourself competing with her. Mama's Boy wants you to do everything his mother does. Next thing you know he's got you wearing Red Cross shoes and polyester stretch pants. He talks you into cutting your hair and dying it blue. Now you and his mom can pass for sisters. His dad ogles you and says, "You got yourself a good woman, Son."

THE SPORTS CHANNEL ZOMBIE

You swore he was alive when you moved in with him. He's sitting in front of the TV clutching the remote control, eyes glazed, barely breathing. His jaw is slack, moving only to catch a handful of pretzels. This could mean he's brain dead. You call an ambulance.

He suddenly throws his fists in the air and shouts, "Yes!"

He's alive. You cancel the ambulance. He glazes over again. You strip naked and pose seductively in front of the TV screen. He points his remote at you and tries to change the channel. You offer him a night of incredible, amazing sex. He breaks wind and falls asleep.

THE NEED MACHINE

It doesn't matter if he's CEO of a Fortune 500 company who juggles complex projects, an expert mechanic or a fearless dog catcher. He needs you to make his toast. He needs you to microwave his cheese sandwich. He whines about his problems and needs you to listen. The Need Machine does most of his whining while he's driving and you're in the passenger seat —and if you're not listening attentively, he turns into a raving mental patient.

The next time he needs to complain about his life while he's driving, ask him to call you from his car phone.

THE MEGALOMANIAC

He talks incessantly about himself. He loves you because the two of you have so much in common: Him. He's a fantastic lover, when he's masturbating.

He calls your answering machine and leaves the following message: "Hi, it's Me. I'll be in Aspen skiing with (famous name here— they *always* name drop) this week. Would you like an opportunity to sleep with me before I leave?"

If you do, he does it like he's doing you a favor. L'amour with The Megalomaniac is a race to the finish line and he always gets there first. You want to race again, but he's already snoring in your ear.

SPONGE MAN

He stays at your place for months and doesn't pitch in for the rent. He uses up your shampoo and razor blades and never buys toilet paper. He eats your last donut.

"You're such a darling," Sponge Man says. "I want to treat you to something special."

He offers to buy you dinner, then asks you to lend him the money.

THE GUY IN THE PERSONAL ADS

You've read a million Personals and they all describe the same guy. You know, the sensitive, caring one who likes long walks, laughter and candlelight dinners in front of a roaring fireplace. He loves movies, music and heart to heart talks with that special woman of any age or race (sex changes OK). Who the hell is this guy and why can't he get a date?

THE TYPE A-HOLE

If you love roller coaster rides but don't have time for amusement parks, the Type A guy will give you the ride of your life. He's fast, intense, and lasts about three minutes on a good night. If you want quality time, he'll suggest an intimate power breakfast, and pencil you in between his six a.m. open heart surgery and nine p.m. racquetball game.

Type As usually make six figures or more, and always worry you're after their money, status and power. Reassure him immediately. Tell him you own controlling shares in Exxon and AT&T.

Type A doesn't make cute, endearing comments, nor is he demonstrative of his affection. If he says something like, "I'm fond of you," he's ready for a meaningful relationship. If he runs a credit check on you—he's ready for marriage.

THE STEROID SWILLER

He strips every ten minutes to cocoa butter his muscles and pluck stray hairs from his freshly shaved chest. He guzzles steroids in the morning, pumps iron all day, and pumps broads all night. On Sundays he starts to shrivel and deflate. He gets edgy waiting for Monday morning.

He'll do anything to get pumped again; a boon if you're a veterinarian.

He loves vets because they prescribe steroids for flea allergies. If you're a vet, he'll show up every week with a Doberman wedged under each arm.

You can have an exciting affair with The Swiller if you don't mind the side effects of steroids. Here's a handy checklist to carry on a date:

- Don't wear white or anything expensive in case he gets nose bleeds.
- Have an ambulance ready if his liver fails.
- Steroids can sometimes cause impotence. Bring a vibrator.

THE HAIR PSYCHOTIC

You're at the movies, raking your fingers through his fabulous hair. You discover some weird ridges and lumps. You wonder if maybe he lives near a radioactive pond and his scalp is riddled with tumors. You're afraid to ask.

Later, in the heat of passion, you grab his hair and notice you're still clutching it on the way to the bathroom.

"Is this yours?" You ask.

"No," he says, tugging on a baseball cap.

"Wasn't this on your head just a minute ago?"

"My, uh, cat coughs up very large hairballs."

The Hair Psychotic is a 'hair club' customer who denies he wears fake hair. If you expose his bald secret, he'll say, "I shave this spot."

"Why don't you shave your *entire* head?" you ask. "Like all the basketball players do."

"Bald is cool, but partial baldness is cooler. The Sean Connery look is the future. Trust me."

THE GREEN CARD SEEKER

He's mysterious, exotic, desperately in love with you, and barely speaks English. You met him yesterday by the coffee machine while waiting to get your tires changed at Sears.

Your hair was greasy, you had PMS and a big red pimple on your nose.

He is not daunted by your lack of glamour.

"You are so *byooo-tee-ful*," he croons.

"You're a moron," you reply.

"Yes," he chuckles.

"I like your honesty. You're very charming."

The Green Card Seeker takes you to McDonald's for dinner and proposes.

After you marry him, a busload of his relatives show up at your door waving their citizenship applications.

THE CROSS DRESSER

He's lustfully eyeing your slinky red cocktail dress.

"Gorgeous," he sighs, moving his hands to your black lace bra. "Can I take this home?"

You surrender your bra to him, thinking he wants to sleep with the scent of you wrapped around his face.

"I love your shoes," he says, removing them. "What size are they?"

"Ten," you reply.

"Such big feet for a woman." He compares his foot to yours. "*We're practically the same size,*" he moans with joy. "We could have a beautiful life together."

Dump him. He just wants to get into your underpants.

THE CLOSET HOMOSEXUAL

He cruises boutiques with you, knows how to accessorize. He's muscular, handsome — too incredible to be true. You haven't slept with him yet and he's already introducing you to his parents, aunts and uncles as his future wife.

"We want to have *lots* of children," he announces.

Flattered, you take him behind a tree and kiss him. He finds you repulsive and pukes. He doesn't have the nerve to tell Mom and Dad he shares a queen sized bed with a hairdresser named Bob. With you on his arm, his relatives won't suspect he's gay.

He only calls to invite you to weddings, funerals and family barbecues.

THE BAD VEGAS ACT

Some men actually believe they're Julio Iglesias. Scientists say it's a genetic defect. They sing at Bingo halls and cocktail lounges. Some claim they were Elvis in a previous life. They croon love songs accompanied by a battery-powered beat box, and they know their voice gets you totally hot and crazy. After their show, they expect you to tear off your clothes and beg for sex. When they're not doing their lounge act, they show up at these locations:

- Singles parties.
- Hotel discos.
- At your door selling carpet cleaning services.

Look out for reproductions of Wayne Newton, Mel Torme, and Tony Bennett. This defect mutates into all forms of Vegas acts.

NAME THAT PENIS

My friends can't understand why men name their penises like they're separate beings.

"Let's see...there was Moe, Larry and Curly...Charlie, Basil, Winston and Junior...Joey, Johnny and Ted," one friend remembered. "I can't recall who the owners of these penises were."

Men like to blame their dicks for things they do wrong.

Has your man accused his penis of anything lately? When he acts as if there's a tiny, evil person living in his undershorts, it just might be true.

Here are some common accusations:

"It wasn't my idea—it was *Curly's*," he says after eloping with his best friend's girl.

"*I'm* willing to go for a vasectomy— *Moe* won't let me."

"I told *Basil* to come home. The bastard wouldn't listen."

"*Winston* didn't call you? I can't believe him!"

MY CAR, MY WEENIE

Maria, who owns a used car dealership, says she can estimate the size of a man's penis by the car he buys. According to Maria, a car is the antithesis of its owner's wiener. If he goes after a long, sleek Corvette he's hung like a peanut. If he buys a Geo Metro he's a regular Paul Bunyan. Average sized guys go after mid-sized cars with lots of options.

R· Piccolo

THE STRANGER IN YOUR KITCHEN

If you want to know your man like you know your best girlfriend, forget it. Men don't readily reveal things about themselves. You can be dating a guy for months, even years before you find out what sort of person he is. You might not find out until after he's dead.

To figure a guy out, invite him to cook a meal with you. The way a man cooks tells a lot about him. Letting him open cans doesn't count, nor does nuking frozen burritos.

Observe the way he chops vegetables. If he slices them into minuscule squares, it indicates he's neat and fastidious. This is great if you're a slob. He'll never feel comfortable in your house unless he cleans it first.

If he color-coordinates every item in the frying pan, juxtaposing light-hued vegetables with dark ones, he thinks too much and lacks spontaneity. In bed, he'll be awkward and predictable.

If he rips open a box of spaghetti with his teeth and tears up the veggies with his bare hands, skip dinner and jump him.

If he shoves everything into the microwave just to get it over with, he'll be a lazy lover. You'll have to do all the work.

If he screams and curses while repeatedly stabbing a head of lettuce, call the cops.

UNSOLVED MYSTERIES

The male mystique has facets we can't explain, raises questions we feebly try to answer.

For instance…

Why do men take out the garbage?

My friend, Kelly, thinks it's because they view themselves as nothing more than garbage men. They compensate for this low self image by acting superior, creating and fighting wars, getting all the good jobs, and monopolizing the sports arenas. I tell her she's overreacting.

"Have you ever seen a garbage *woman?*" she asked. "I'll bet you a hundred bucks you'll never see a garbage collector with tits."

"They all have tits." I said.

"But they're guy-tits." she said. "The superior sex would *never* haul trash, no matter how much it pays."

"What's the starting salary?" I asked.

"Fifty grand a year with medical and dental benefits, yearly raises and early retirement."

I want to quit my job and head straight for the sanitation department.

Why do they barbecue?

A psychoanalyst I know is currently researching what she calls The Barbecue Phenomenon. This is when a man refuses to cook, claims he can do nothing more than boil water, and doesn't actually know where the kitchen is located in his own house. Yet he MUST barbecue. When the decision is made to cook outdoors, he's wielding lighter fluid and throwing chickens on the grill with a crazed look in his eyes.

"He's very possessive of the barbecue—he won't let me near it," one of the subject's wives commented. "I tried to grill my own burger and he threatened me with a spatula."

"It's a primal need," said the psychoanalyst. "It stems from a time when cave men had to light fires to survive."

Donna, a heavy smoker, agreed. "Guys are always offering to light my cigarettes," she said, "with their lighter cranked up to torch."

"I remember that about John," I said of an ex-boyfriend.

"I remember those huge flames quivering from his Zippo lighter, stopping inches from my lips."

"I thought you didn't smoke!" she said.

"I don't. He was just obsessed with lighters." After we broke up, he married a fire eater.

THE MEN'S MOVEMENT

-R. Piccolo-

Why do men read in the bathroom?

Debbie and Andrea wonder why men carry reading material into the bathroom and vanish for hours.

"At first I thought aliens came and took him away," Debbie confessed. "When I knocked on the door I couldn't believe he was still in there."

"That's nothing," Andrea replied. "My husband's in there every day from nine to five. For years I thought he was operating a business from our bathroom."

"Steve keeps a stack of encyclopedias next to his toilet," Debbie complained.

"That's nothing," Andrea retorted. "Dave has cable TV and a fax machine next to his."

"I don't get it. Why would anyone spend leisure time in the bathroom if they're not taking a bath?" Debbie asked.

"Men differ," Andrea pointed out. "They enjoy hanging out in small rooms like tool sheds and wine cellars. It makes them feel snug and secure. Men seek snugness."

"Why?"

"Maybe it's because they wear baggy clothes," she speculated. "Think about the clothes they wear to work. Suits, coveralls, jeans that droop. How can they feel snug and secure in loose clothing?"

"So you're saying that men spend too much time in the bathroom because their pants aren't tight enough?"

"Exactly."

Why do they leave piles of change everywhere?

Other things perplex us.

Karen asked, "When they unload their pockets, why do they leave their change all over the place?"

"Loose clothes again," Andrea said, fixated on her brilliant personal hypothesis. "Those coins jingle around in their pockets all day like Chinese water torture and it makes them irritable. As soon as they dump their change, they're fine."

"Bob leaves it all over the place," Karen griped. "There were pennies and dimes in the meat loaf last night."

Why get annoyed? Collect his change and save it. Soon you'll be able to purchase that mink coat he never bought you. Take the cruise he was too cheap to spring for. Drive across country breezing through toll machines. Run for Governor! One grandmother saved enough quarters to retire in front of a slot machine at Trump Castle.

GUILT TRIPS

Diane called at three in the morning.

"I'm on a guilt trip," she said.

"You'd better be. For calling me at three in the friggin' morning."

"Sorry about the time difference —I'm in Fiji having lunch," she went on. "Tony acted like an asshole last week. He feels guilty, so he's taking me on a tour of the South Pacific."

Diane takes guilt trips whenever she has a fight with her boyfriend *du jour*. She sobs and berates him until he's racked with shame. Then he'll do anything to get off her shit list.

"Men thrive in a state of guilt," she says. "To get the most out of a man, act as if you dislike him. If you're too nice, he'll hate you for it. He'll irritate you until you get pissed off enough to make him feel guilty again."

I take Diane's advice when I go out with my mother, who always looks wistful when she sees a guy carrying roses.

"Isn't that sweet," she sighs.

"He did something to piss off his wife," I reply.

"He's the man I should have married," my mother says, eyeing his Rolex. "I wish your father would bring me roses."

"You should treat him like dirt more often," I say. "You'll never get flowers being loving and tolerant. Men need abuse, trust me. They appreciate you more when they're plagued with guilt."

My mother started thinking. "Hmmm...I took your father's car to the service station and he never thanked me for it."

"When?"

"Fifteen years ago."

"Don't let him forget it, ever!" I steer her to a pay phone. "Call him right now and tell him how disappointed and angry you feel about it. Tell him how inconsiderate he was, recount the vivid details of that hateful day."

"I'll ask for a divorce," she says, still eyeing the Rolex.

"Threaten you'll leave him if he doesn't apologize," I say. "Then give him your travel agent's phone number."

Guilt can be costly. If your man spends money to soothe his nagging conscience (you), make sure he doesn't waste it on a shrink. Your life would be unbearably tranquil if you shared it with a normal, well adjusted being.

Don't worry if he doesn't have money. Keep a list of personal services he could provide. Maybe you could use a guilt paint-job for the house, a guilt car wash, guilt dog walk, or guilt massage.

No matter what a guy does to disrupt your life, you can guilt him into doing whatever it takes to make your bitter heart sweet again. Have fun. Get creative. Ask him to use his vacation to watch the kids while you spend a month at that Zen retreat you always wanted to check out. If he's an electronics whiz, ask him to build you a robot that vibrates. Is he a lawyer? Make him sue your hairdresser for that bad hair cut you suffered from. There's nothing your man wouldn't do to get you to like him again.

FASHION CASUALTIES

Dawn, a fashion designer, told a frightening story.

"I was dizzy, nauseous—I thought I was having flashbacks from the acid someone slipped in my beer back in '72. I saw pink and white stripes and little green greyhounds floating on a sea of red. I saw orange suede loafers, plaid socks and blue linen slacks. I wasn't hallucinating. I was looking at my husband's clothes," she said.

"He was going out with *me* dressed like *that*. He was all tarted up in a pink striped shirt his ex-wife bought, a greyhound print tie his mother gave him for Christmas, and a pair of two hundred dollar slacks that I bought him, hoping I could leave the house with a decent looking man for a change. With his expensive slacks, he wears orange suede loafers from the sale rack at K-Mart." Dawn was visibly upset.

"He was so excited about those shoes. He got them at a real bargain and he insisted on wearing them. I mean, I could have forgiven his entire getup, but the shoes were for two left feet!"

If you're buying clothes for your man thinking he'll look coordinated and stylish, don't waste your money. He'll mix and mismatch the stuff you bought with everything his mother and ex-girlfriends bought for him. A man's wardrobe represents the notion of how he should look according to every woman he knows. He selects indiscriminately from anything that's clean.

Going out with a man who actually *wears* the tasteless gifts he receives can be embarrassing. He gets loud, chaotic ties on every holiday except Ground Hog Day, and sweaters that only look good on mannequins. He might wear these nasty accouterments to a dance club with cheap cologne he gets for his birthday, and a gold plated golf tee that doubles as a tie clip.

If this happens, never say, "I want you to dress cool."

He might wear the golf tee as an earring.

A man's objective should be to look like the guys in GQ. This fashion Mecca for men—

where hunky models with pissed off, constipated expressions, sport the latest styles—makes you want to refinance your house so you could buy your man Armani suits. Forget this notion. Consider trading him for a GQ model. Who cares if he looks pissed off and constipated? He's wearing hot clothes. And you didn't have to buy them.

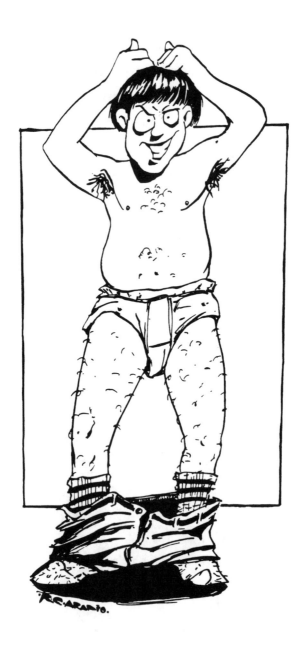

I'M TOO SEXY FOR MY BAGGY, WHITE FRUIT OF THE LOOM BRIEFS

Women can't have sex unless they feel sexy. This involves a shower, perfume, pedicure, feminine spray, firm thighs, overpriced undies from Victoria's Secret, and breath mints.

Men don't need this preamble to get laid. They feel sexy all the time. It doesn't matter if he's just been out back filling the trough with pig slop, he ate garlic flavored beef jerky for lunch, and he has enough gas to fly to Mars and back—he's ready for **L-O-V-E.**

If you just met him, he's probably shaving, splashing on cologne and wearing bikini underwear. When he realizes he'll be sleeping with you whether he grooms or not, he will disregard these pre-coital rituals. The only time he *won't* be ready for sex is right after he has an orgasm and you didn't. In this case, wait twenty minutes. Change your hairstyle and lingerie. Proceed as usual.

UNSOLVED RELATIONSHIPS

One of my friends who's been married for twenty years teaches an adult education course called *How to Stay Married*. Hundreds of people sign up wanting to know how to stay interested in someone they're terminally bored with.

She tells her students, "My husband and I have never gotten bored. We always make love the instant we see each other."

She doesn't mention that her husband's been living in China for the past ten years.

I took her course twice, thinking I missed something. I reviewed the notes, hand-outs, and edible panties. I bought Jack Hammer, Boy Blow-up Doll, and practiced all the exercises. I dumped my second husband for Jack. As I signed the divorce papers, I wondered if anyone was teaching a course on *How To Become a Lesbian*.

I was watching my ex gather his belongings when I remembered our first date. As he packed up his nachos and beer I thought, if every day was like our first date, we'd still be attracted to each other.

We were both so glamorous that night. His acid washed jeans fit perfectly. So did mine. He reeked of Halston, I reeked of Obsession. He had long, sexy eyelashes and so did I — from six coats of waterproof, lash-builder, heavy artillery mascara. I could sleep for weeks in it and never wake up with smudges.

I felt confident until I discovered how much fresher he looked than I did in the morning. I woke up and tried not to breathe in his direction. He rolled over and smiled. His hair wasn't mangled, his eyes weren't stuck together, his breath even smelled minty.

If I married this guy and wanted to look as good as him, I'd have to wear waterproof mascara for the rest of my life. I'd have to wake up at dawn every morning to blow-dry so he won't see me with flat hair. Crush proof hair spray doesn't exist, so I'm screwed. Maybe he'd fall in love with me and turn into a belching, beer-chugging, flatulent slob like so many other guys my friends and I had known. Until then, I'd look hot in the morning. I'd set the alarm for five a.m., get up before he does and freshen up.

One morning while sneaking out of bed, I bumped into him in the hall. We raced for the blow dryer. He grabbed it first.

"Are you always up this early?" I asked as he slammed the bathroom door in my face. I thought I saw one of his eyes stuck shut.

"I'm a morning person," he answered.

He returned to bed with perfect hair, sparkling teeth and Brute-scented armpits. I took Polaroids of him.

When a guy tries this hard, you need a souvenir. You know those gallant efforts won't last, because first dates are...

THE LUNAR ECLIPSES OF LOVE

In the beginning, a guy goes to great lengths to get laid. He splurges on dinners at posh restaurants, makes you feel as if you've known him all your life.

Occasionally, I find myself on a date with the man of my dreams. He reveals his deepest secrets, his deepest fears. I'm instantly intrigued. He doesn't believe in sex. He believes in seduction. I'm instantly in love. I'm certain he's *the one.*

I look at the same guy six months later. He's wearing a Metallica T-shirt with ketchup stains on it and no underwear. He shakes his weenie at me, smiling like he's Pat Sajak and I'm a *Wheel of Fortune* champ about to go for the big spin.

"Look what I got for you," he says, pointing at his crotch. I'm instantly ready to scarf down a pizza, a pint of Häagen Dazs and a bag of chips.

Love fades. I don't know how it happens. My friend who's been married for twenty years is getting rich from a book she just wrote called, *How to Walk Around Naked and Get Him to Notice You're in the Room.*

Not all relationships degenerate. If you go after wonderful guys who have the ability to remain wonderful, you have a good chance of getting laid at fifty. If you fall for intractable morons who should donate their frontal lobes to science while they're still alive, you'll have to take up knitting. How can you tell if you're in love with a loser? Here are some warning signs:

- His recycling bins are filled with condoms.
- He gargles with Bud Light.
- He gets more hate mail from ex-girlfriends than junk mail.
- He has 57 cents in his checking account.
- He forgot how many times he was married.
- Carloads of kids show up at his house every Sunday shouting, "Daddy! Daddy!"
- He dries his socks in the microwave.
- His address book has nothing but "900" numbers in it.

Fortunately, nature has blessed women with keen intuition. When you realize you're dating or marrying the wrong guy, an alarm goes off in your head. Unfortunately, nature made the alarm silent, so you can't hear it.

MARRIAGE OR BUST

Living in sin was cool until they changed the tax laws. Couples all over the nation suddenly said, "Honey, before we have that third kid we always wanted, let's do something crazy—let's get married!"

Everyone decided *The Brady Bunch* was a sign from God. If we didn't become Mike and Carol Brady we'd be miserable, unfulfilled fools, missing out on tax shelters.

Marriage can be rewarding if you do it for the right reasons.

Reasons you should marry him *immediately:*

- He just won the lottery.
- He never leaves the toilet seat up.
- He adores cellulite.
- He can bear children and breast feed.
- He's in the fashion business and knows where the sample sales are.
- Calvin Klein is his close, personal friend.
- He has a fabulous body and hates wearing anything other than a towel.

These are the *wrong* reasons to marry:

- He has a British accent and can imitate your favorite rock star.
- His last name is Trump — no relation to Donald.
- He can fix your car.
- He has everything except hair and a personality.
- You want to change your last name to his because no one can pronounce, spell or remember yours.
- You're lonely and desperate, he has a pulse.
- He's a fascinating, tortured artist.
- He reminds you of your father.
- He's the guy you had a crush on in high school who never knew you were alive— and still doesn't.

A DIVORCE MADE IN HELL

Joanne is always a mess. Every time I call her she's either falling in love, marrying or divorcing someone. Whenever she marries a jerk, her parents order her not to divorce him. They believe love is forever and she should heed the vows: For better or worse, till death do you part—and they paid fifty grand for the wedding. The people who shelled out 150 bucks for prime rib and wedding cake were really pissed.

Her lawyer was thrilled.

She's filing for her third divorce, and *Modern Bride* magazine just offered her a lifetime subscription.

Divorce number one went something like this:

"I'm taking the kids!" her ex shouted first.

"We don't have kids," she said.

"Then I'm taking the dog."

After she paid her lawyer she announced, "I'm taking the dog, the furniture and half your pay check."

All was well until she married the next guy, who couldn't hold a job and went broke.

Divorce number two went like this:

"I'm taking the kids!" he shouted.

"Oh yeah? Who's going to take care of them while you're job hunting?"

"You are," he said.

"You're taking the dog. I'm taking the kids," she said.

A bitter custody battled ensued.

Her lawyer racked up more bucks.

In the end, she got the kids, the kids got the dog, her ex got to file bankruptcy.

Joanne discovered that raising kids alone sucks, so she's willing to search for another partner. She found the third man of her dreams.

He had six kids and a dog, but so what? He was sexy and handsome and caring, and his annual net income was a half million dollars.

He bought her a huge, gorgeous house, adopted her two children, and hired a nanny to take care of them. His kids hate her, but so what? She couldn't have found a more perfect man.

Shortly after the honeymoon he fell in love with the nanny, and ran off with her.

There's a button on Joanne's phone that automatically dials her lawyer.

Divorce number three ensued.

"I'm *leaving* the kids!" he shouted.

"Oh, no. They're *your* kids—you take them!" she demanded.

"Take the dogs too!"

He laughed.

She issued the final order.

"I want the house, the Mercedes, and the horses."

"If you want the house, you have to take everything that's in it," he said. "Including the kids and the dogs!"

"And your money," she replied.

She figured the sooner he got out of her life, the sooner she could start a new one. She took the bastard for every cent he had. All he has to show for his life now is a 23-year-old girlfriend and no responsibilities. She has enough money to feed her horses, put eight kids through college, send the dogs to a shrink for emotionally damaged canines, and buy an Uzi to blow her ex-husband's brains out.

A GLOBAL VIEW

I always assumed that perfectly normal, well behaved males turn into gibbering idiots the minute they see a pair of exposed breasts. This, of course, doesn't happen if he sees *your* breasts, or say, a pair of breasts in *National Geographic.* Sometimes he only needs to see ample cleavage in order to regress to the age of seven.

European men I've dated argue that boobophiles only exist in America.

Jean-Claude, the Frenchman, puffed his cigarette looking bored as we sat on a crowded beach in the South of France, where the only person wearing a bathing suit top was me.

"Breasts, who cares? You see them everywhere," he said as if he were an African tribesman. "Big, small—what's the big deal, eh?"

Finally, reluctantly, I took off my bathing suit top. I started feeling uncomfortable. No men were ogling me. Not even my boyfriend.

"American men would get boners at this beach," I remarked.

"They are stupid," he said with disgust.

"They go ape-shit over lingerie too," I said. "They get horny looking at panty advertisements."

"Ridiculous."

"Sexy lingerie doesn't excite you?"

"The French wear it every day. So common." He lit another cigarette. "Very boring."

I cursed myself for spending too much money on that blue lace teddy I wore the other night. He had looked at me as if I were wearing overalls.

"What does excite *you* French?" I asked.

He leered. "What excites the French?" He exhaled smoke rings. "Angry women."

"What does an angry woman have to do to turn you on?"

"Smash dishes. Curse. We love it," he said.

"You'd get aroused if I threw a tantrum?"

"I would become foolish, idiotic—like a schoolboy. I would make passionate love to you every day and every night for a week."

"And at the end of the week?"

"You would have to smash more dishes."

Why was I buying lingerie when I should have been buying china?

Englishmen seem less foreign. There's no language barrier. But they still tell you things that mean something completely different. For example, Nigel, a British guy I dated once said, "I'm going out for cigarettes. I'll be right back." He returned three days later.

"Where the hell were you?" I asked.

Uncertain, he replied, "Stopped at the pub for a bit."

"You've been sitting in a bar for three days?"

"Has it been three days?" He looked at his watch. "I thought my bladder felt rather full."

I lived in England until I grew tired of Nigel, who belonged to a pack of pub-going, tea-swilling, butt-smoking lads who criticized Americans for being excessive and having bad taste. Nigel was right. Living in England *was* excessive, and by dating him, I was exemplifying bad taste.

I returned to America to argue with my own kind. American men have an edge over Englishmen. Only a slight one, though. When an American guy says, "I'll be right back," he doesn't disappear for three days. He disappears for three hours. So if you order a pizza and you're ravenous, don't send him to pick it up.

If an Englishmen leaves the house on an errand and never returns, it's safe to assume he's been sucked into the Bermuda Triangle of British culture: the pub. But where do American men go when you're expecting them to walk through the door any moment, for hours on end?

Kelly said, "My first thought is always: *he's seeing another woman.* I drive myself crazy with jealousy. Who she? Are her thighs thinner than mine? I'll kick her skinny butt!"

I told Kelly about my latest flame, Tony. "He's been great so far, but I have to admit, whenever he disappears, I'm wondering if he's seeing somebody else too."

One morning, Tony went to the corner store to get some butter.

"I'll be right back," he promised.

"I'm putting two slices of bread in the toaster," I said. "When they're toast, you'd better be back here with butter."

He returned three hours later with a trunk full of groceries and a pair of skis.

"I found a discount warehouse," he said excitedly. "The food's real cheap—and they sell sporting goods too!" He brought in a box from the car and tore it open.

"Look at this vintage Elvis outfit I found!" He flashed white sequined bell bottoms at me. "I bet he actually wore this at his last concert. Look, it still has peanut butter stains on it!"

"Where's the butter?" I asked, using my fossilized toast as a doorstop.

"I got something better." He handed me a hunk of neon-yellow lard. "It's less than half the price of butter," he said proudly. "So I bought a case."

Rule: If you need something, get it yourself. Men with wanderlust lose focus the second they leave their environment and enter a store. They forget their purpose, and shop every isle for all the unnecessary junk they can find. The only time he buys the first thing he sees—then promptly rushes out of the store—is when he shops for your birthday present.

DEAR OLD DAD

My father, who is of Italian descent, has been an American citizen for the past forty years and still can't speak proper English.

Italians believe women should remain virgins until their wedding day. To protect their virginity, daughters are forbidden to move out of the house.

My father told me I could leave home under one of two conditions: If I got married or if I died. He wanted me to tie the knot before I turned thirty.

"Women are like cheese," he said. "If it gets old, the mice don't want it no more."

This was a lesson on how to catch a man.

The trouble was, my father never approved of my boyfriends. He hated them all.

"I don't like him," he said when I introduced him to Erik, the tall, blonde football player who towered a full twelve inches over my father's head. "When I talk to a man, I wanna look him in the eye, not in the fly."

That left me with a choice of midgets. I brought one home.

"I don't like him," Dad said. "He's not Italian. Marry a nice Italian boy."

"I don't know any Italian midgets," I said.

"What about Rocco? He's a nice boy."

Rocco, my mother's friend's cousin's godson who has lived next door since I was two, is about five feet one, drives a red Corvette with tractor wheels, and can't speak proper English. He's been in America since he was born.

He has a back yard pool with a diving board and was always showing off. Every morning he'd be out there jettisoning into the water. One day he forgot to take off his gold jewelry and sank to the bottom.

So much for Rocco.

"How about Dino?" my old man nagged.

"The Flintstones' dinosaur?"

"Rocco's brother."

Dino was the same as Rocco, only he was older and wore heavier jewelry. To appease Dad, I agreed to go out with Dino. His father and my father got together and made a deal.

It went something like, Dino had to buy me a ring and a house, and I had to keep my legs closed until the wedding.

On our first date, Dino took me to the track.

He spent the whole afternoon jumping out of his seat either to dash to the betting booth or to shout at his horse until it finished the race. When his horse won, he'd throw his arm around me and squeeze me. Every time he grabbed me, his bracelet left dents in my shoulder. When he hugged me, his big, diamond studded, 18 carat gold crucifix of Christ in a thorny crown gouged me in the chest.

I came home covered with bruises.

My father put a contract out on him.

Finally the day came when I thought I found Mr. Right. He seemed like he was everything my old man wanted. He was short, Italian and rich, and was never indicted for anything.

"What does he do?" Dad asked.

"Nothing. His parents are wealthy," I said. "He doesn't have to work for the rest of his life."

"No job? I don't like that."

"Marry him," my mother commanded.

The old man shrugged. "You gotta respect your mother's wishes."

We set a wedding date and invited two hundred people.

I invited a hundred friends and relatives. He invited ten relatives and ninety body guards. We would spend our honeymoon in Acapulco, Mexico.

It was a lovely wedding. Everyone wished us well, gave us cash and ate like pigs at the reception. I ordered a buffet dinner forgetting my relatives would bring shopping bags full of Tupperware and load them up with food to take home. After dinner and cake, they turned off the lights and wheeled out the flaming Viennese cart. It was piled with exotic deserts of every kind. I never found out what kind they were. My relatives ravaged the cart before the spotlights went on. When the waiter presented the table to my in-laws, the only thing left was a chocolate cannoli with teeth marks on it.

I didn't care. I had a husband my father approved of. At last, he'd stop nagging me to get married. When the guests left, I asked him what he thought of his new son-in-law.

"I know a good divorce lawyer," he said. "Call him when you get to Mexico."

THE WEDDING PARTY HAD SUDDENLY RUN OUT OF RICE.

DAD SQUARED

My girlfriend, Jennifer, complains, "I always go out with guys who have personality traits like my father. Am I nuts?"

"It's common. A lot of women do it."

Psychologists say women are often attracted to men who behave like their earliest role model—usually their father.

Another friend, Robin, disagrees. "My Dad passed away when I was four. How could I have married a guy like my father if I never knew him?"

"Your earliest role model could have been a man who had significant influence on you. Who did you admire as a child?"

"Batman," she said.

"There you have it. Batman works at home and so does your husband."

"I never told you this," Robin said. "He wears purple tights and a cape when he works."

"Does he have a Batmobile?"

"He drives an Audi." Robin pondered the issue. "But come to think of it, Bruce *is* a lot like Batman. Why didn't I realize it?"

According to psychologists, your attraction to men comes from a strong, subconscious level. Most of the time you're attracted to men who seem familiar.

If you first meet a man whom you feel you've known all your life, chances are, you have. You can tell your man is too much like Dad if he...

- Claims exclusive rights to the chair in front of the television.
- Tells the same stories over and over, even if you've heard them a million times.
- Gives you money for your birthday, then tells you what to buy with it.
- Acts like the money he gave you is still his.
- Won't let you take the car without him in it.
- Snores so loud the furniture shakes.
- Doesn't know how to operate a washing machine.
- Expounds on subjects he knows nothing about, trying to give the impression he's an expert.
- Eats a lot of bran, enjoys a good BM.

good sex

great sex

good bowel movement

BOY TALK

Elaine's story:

What do men talk about when women aren't around? Do they swap shaving secrets? Do they pour their hearts out like women do? Do they talk blatantly about their sex lives like all Elaine's friends do?

Needing to know, Elaine called a private investigator...

"My husband is hosting a poker game Friday night," she said. "I want you to set up a hidden microphone near the table so I can hear what the guys say to each other."

The investigator, whom she calls "Dick" asked, "You think your husband's having an affair?"

"He's having a bunch of guys over."

"It's an excuse to get you out of the house," Dick said. "I'll put a camera in the bedroom."

"I just want to know what guys talk about when women aren't around," she said.

"Right. If he tells his buddies he's cheating—you got proof."

"I want the poker table bugged," she said. "I'm doing a study of the male mind. When I find results I'm going on *Donahue*."

"How about if I throw a camera in the bedroom, no charge."

"Free? Okay, what the heck."

Who could refuse something free?

Following the poker game, Dick brought the tapes over. He showed Elaine the video tape from the bedroom first. She watched her cat, Spanky, biting himself on the bed for twenty minutes.

"He needs a flea collar," Dick said.

"Is this all that happened in the bedroom?"

"Yeah, but I left the camera in there, just in case."

They listened to the poker game tape. Elaine was giddy with curiosity. Her husband, Rick, and his buddies, Steve, Joe and Tom, were spewing boy-talk. And she was eavesdropping on their sacred domain!

They talked poker. They said stuff like, "your deal," "raise you five," and "I'm out."

"Fast-forward to the juicy stuff!" she ordered.

Dick did as he was told. "Here it is. This is where they get intimate."

"How about those Mets?" Elaine heard Rick say.

"They suck," his friend, Steve, replied. "They're in last place."

"Who are you betting on this year for the series?"

Elaine was getting impatient. "Where's the good stuff?"

"This is *it*," Dick said.

"I don't want to hear sports talk! Where's the revealing stuff?"

"You have to understand," he said. "When a man talks sports, he's communicating something deeper. For example, the guy who said *the Mets suck* is really saying he's having trouble with his wife."

"Are you sure?"

"Absolutely. You have to read between the lines."

"My husband said 'How about those Mets?' What does *that* mean?"

"He was asking his friend how he was getting along with his wife."

Dick played more tape.

"I'm betting on the Yanks," Joe commented.

"What does that mean?" Elaine asked.

"He's worried about his prostate gland."

"They always blow it in the ninth inning," Tom said. "I'm going for the Red Sox."

"He's upset," the detective interpreted.

"About what?"

"He wants kids but he can't score a girlfriend. Women keep dumping him."

"I want the Sox to kick ass this year," Tom went on.

"He wants to move to Saudi Arabia," Dick translated. "Women aren't allowed to dump men there."

According to Dick, here's what Elaine's husband and his pals said, and here's what they meant:

STATEMENT

"Baseball is for assholes."

"I bet the Giants will
take the Superbowl."

"Belch."

"Pass the chips."

"The Cowboys took the Bills last year.
I lost 25 bucks on that game."

"They turned over every offensive."

"The QB got sacked."

"Dallas has some great knockers
on the side line."

MEANING

"I'm having a mid-life crisis and
my wife is in Florida."

"I feel guilty about my
sexual fantasies. I can't screw my wife
unless I think about a French maid
driving a lawn mower."

"Belch."

"I'm afraid I'll die of a heart attack."

"Hot weather makes my nuts sag.
I find that upsetting."

"I love little black cocktail dresses.
I wish I had the guts to wear one."

"Get away from me, you homo."

"Women are lucky. If I could wear a
long dress with no underwear on
a breezy day, my balls would be happy."

STATEMENT

"Ruth gives the best blow jobs."

"You said your ex-girlfriend gave the best blow jobs."

"I'm a happily married man."

"Me too. Nothing better than a good marriage and a steady paycheck."

MEANING

"I'm deeply in love."

"I hope your penis isn't
bigger than mine.

"I'm so repulsive I'd have to pay for sex
if I wasn't married."

"If I can't afford to get hog-tied and
spanked once a month by
Mistress Olga, I'll shoot myself."

Elaine learned from this dialogue. She learned that men really do bare their souls, and they're not the basal, superficial creatures she thought they were.

"Thanks for translating," she said to Dick.

"I'm charging you extra for it," he said. "Call me when you're gonna be on *Donahue* so I can tell everyone I know you."

STANLEY IS UNABLE TO PLAY GOLF
BECAUSE HE CAN'T FIND HIS BALLS

NECESSARY OBJECTS

When you marry a man, you marry his stuff. There are things men must carry through life; things they never use but keep for no apparent reason. If you have to share storage space with a guy, prepare to get less space for your things due to the stuff he stuffs in your space.

BALLS

In the trunk of his car you'll find a football, basketball, baseball, bowling ball or a shitload of golf balls. You'll find them in the closet or the TV room, should he need to play with his balls while watching the sports channel. Seldom will you find him using these balls in actual sports games.

As men get older their balls get heavier. When he's born, his Dad buys him a baseball. He enters adolescence, he gets a football. When he's twenty he buys himself a basketball. At thirty, he buys a bowling ball. At forty, he gets a hernia from lifting the bowling ball, then discovers golf.

His first game of golf is a religious experience. Little, white light-as-a-feather balls give him the thrill of his life. He can own dozens. They're so small he can play with them indoors!

Your house becomes golf ball land. The kitchen drawer where you shove stuff you don't know what to do with is now filled with golf balls. They're in the china closet, the fruit bowl—they're rolling off the refrigerator.

He rips out the carpet and installs astro-turf. He turns your den into a nine hole putting green. Your back yard becomes a driving range. Flocks of geese show up thinking it's a place to lay eggs.

If you can't cope, give him an ultimatum. Say, "It's either me or your balls." You might risk losing him, though. No matter what size, shape, or amount, a man's gotta have balls.

CATCHER'S MITT

You wish he would throw out the catcher's mitt he's been hoarding since eighth grade. It's molding and looks like a truck ran over it. You can't understand why he tells you this thing that resembles dried road kill is a sports accessory. He claims he uses it. For what, he won't say.

His other sports accessories double as weapons. He keeps a baseball bat under his bed should he get attacked in his sleep, and a polo mallet in the car in case he needs to fight over a parking space.

His football helmet is a receptacle for odd socks. He uses his lacrosse stick to skim leaves out of the pool.

But what use does this catcher's mitt have other than occupy space where you could be storing one of your 150 pairs of shoes? If he had two mitts, you could fashion them into avant-garde slippers. You'll feel less annoyed about the space that miserable mitt is hogging if you find a use for it.

Here are some ways to utilize that
old catcher's mitt:

- Loan it to the zoo, where lonely
  armadillos can mate with it.
- Wear it to hail taxis during rush hour.
- Offer it to your dog while begging him
  not to chew your furniture.
- Convert it into a door knocker; have it
  bronzed and bolted to your front door.
- Fill it with cement, attach a chain to it,
  and ask your mother-in-law to wear it the
  next time she goes swimming.

3 Things you can do with old catcher's Mitts..!

FASHIONABLE
LEATHER SLIPPERS!

OVEN-MITTS!

DOG-POOP
SCOOPER!

R. Piccolo

PHALLIC HUNTING GEAR

Men who need to kill cute, furry creatures own rifles. They go hunting and return with bloody, disgusting dead things you're supposed to be impressed with. Other guys collect rifles so they can display them and get boners imagining themselves on horseback sprinting across the field on a fox hunt.

"According to Freud," my shrink friend, Carolyn, said, "these men feel the need to conquer. Rifles are metaphors for penises."

In other words, a man feels powerful if he knows he can kill a moose with his penis.

"My boyfriend collects fishing poles," I said.

"Fishing gratifies in a different way," Carolyn said. "Men associate poles with display. Fishing fulfills his exhibitionist needs. He feels powerful when he holds the pole out in front of him for everyone to see."

If fishing fulfills his exhibitionist needs, and he doesn't fish, would he become a flasher? *Nahh.* What do shrinks know? In case she's right, I bought him a tackle box for his birthday instead of that trench coat he wanted.

MUSICAL INSTRUMENTS

Lori's story:

She once lived in a 600-square-foot studio apartment with a boyfriend who owned a drum set that took up half the room.

"Why can't you get a harmonica?" she complained. "Then we can eat on a table."

He shook his head. "I need drums."

"You never play them!"

"I will...when I get time."

The dust mites on his drums grew into dust mice, and then into dust rats, and she never heard a sound.

The last guy she lived with had an electric guitar. He knew the first eight chords of *Smoke on the Water*, and nothing else. He played them over and over until she demanded he learn an entire song or she'd move out. He learned twelve chords of *Stairway to Heaven* and promised he'd figure out the rest if she stayed.

They have two kids and a mortgage now and he still can't play a whole song. Thinking he really wanted to play music but needed motivation, she suggested an idea.

"Why don't you buy a banjo and play it for the kids? They love banjo music."

He want pale. He looked suicidal.

"How would *you* react if you saw me playing that instrument?" he asked. "Would you get hot for my body?"

Lori pictured her husband strumming a banjo and found him totally revolting.

This is why the instruments rock stars play are the only ones a man will keep in his house. He loves to imagine himself on stage, playing in front of thousands of creaming, screaming women. That's why he owns drums or a guitar, not an accordion. Of course, there are exceptions to the rule. A hundred years ago polkas got women all hot and frisky. So if your husband or boyfriend is about 90 years old, an accordion will transform this man into an Olympian sex god.

DISCO HITS
OF THE 70'S TAPE

No matter what age your man is, he'll posses a Disco Hits of the 70s Tape to remind him of a time when guys could wear goofy platform shoes and loud, polyester shirts and get laid every night. He could score with the woman he was making out with on the dance floor before finding out her name.

Ah yes...those were the days, when life was one big disco-sex party. If you got crabs, you could exterminate them. If you got VD, you could take penicillin. Celebrities never gave concerts to benefit herpes. It was a reckless age of innocence. You could die of a drug overdose, but you couldn't die from sex.

Men get all misty when they listen to Donna Summer groaning, *Love to Love You, Baby*. I've seen a guy actually break down and cry when her moans of pleasure filled the air. They just don't make music like that anymore. When was the last time you heard a song that sounded like some woman was getting her brains fucked out?

Remembering the 70s is soothing to a man. It comforts him to know there was a time he could abuse his body without worrying, boff strangers without fear or guilt, and go out dancing in a white polyester suit. Now if he wants to wear white polyester, he has to become a male nurse or drive an ice cream truck.

CIGARS

A small percentage of men habitually smoke cigars. The rest keep a box at home should a special occasion arise and they need to hand them out to a bunch of other guys and smoke in unison. The stench is bad enough when one cigar is lit, but why would they light up twelve at a time? Do men get sincere pleasure from sucking these stink-rolls? Or do they pretend to enjoy it—like we pretend we don't mind if they kiss us with that foul taste on their lips?

ARNOLD SCHWARZENEGGER MOVIES

He has every movie Arnie ever made—even bootleg copies of his early "art" films and Mr. Universe competitions. For every woman who'd love to be Maria Shriver, there are thousands more men who wish they were Arnold. The cocky, rich superstar with the nerdy name appeals to millions of people, no matter what he does. Men love him because he smokes cigars. When a wealthy, muscle-bound superstar lights up a stogie, nobody minds the stink.

POPULAR MYTHS

Men are often judged unfairly. Myths are responsible for unreasonable beliefs we adopt toward them. The next time you catch yourself calling him a stupid, insensitive shit, think twice. You could be all wrong about him.

Note these popular myths:

Men never show emotion

Not true. If you smash his car into a phone pole, he'll wail and sob like an Italian aunt at a funeral.

To win a man's trust, you must reveal your deepest feelings to him

Totally bogus. The more you reveal about yourself, the more he's convinced you're his ex-girlfriend who screwed him over and left him an emotional cripple. Don't tell him anything about yourself—not even your name. He'll just get paranoid.

Men hate to shop

A profound misconception. They love to shop, about every twenty years. We women could love an outfit we bought one day and hate it a week later. But when a man buys, he buys for keeps. He wears his clothes until they disintegrate. When there's nothing left of them, he'll head for the mall.

Where were you when Kennedy was shot? My guy was shopping for a bathrobe. He still wears it, and I keep thinking there's a homeless person shuffling into the bathroom every morning. If you hate watching your man traipse around the house in underwear he bought when he was twenty pounds lighter, sagging socks from which his big toe protrudes, and his Mickey Mouse pajamas that aren't cute anymore, do him a favor—wash them in hydrochloric acid.

He will *never* admit he's wrong

An utter lie. A man will readily and shamefully admit he's wrong when he discovers you've packed up and moved out.

He won't see a doctor until he's at the brink of death

Nonsense. Men see doctors all the time—telepathically. While he's inhaling a bacon-cheese burger slathered with mayo, he sees a doctor in his mind's eye.

"Too much fat in your diet can lead to a fatal heart attack," warns the doctor.

He buys a roast chicken and carefully removes the skin. He eats the skin. He throws out the chicken. On the way home, he scarfs down a hot dog and an ice cream.

As he doubles over with gas pain, he feels a sharp jab in his chest. He closes his eyes and sees the doctor. The doctor is handing him a bill for two hundred bucks. What a rip off! Two hundred bucks to find out he has high cholesterol and irritable bowels! He decides he will never see this doctor again.

The truth is, men don't enjoy spending money on intangible things like "health." If they walk into a doctor's office, they want to come out with something to show for it. They won't get an annual check-up unless the doctor can guarantee them an illness—or at least a bottle of pills.

THE DELUXE HIGH-CHOLESTEROL HEART-ATTACK
TRIPLE-DECKER 6-PATTY GREASE-DRIPPING
MEGA-FAT POUND-O-CHEESE BLOOD-CLOTTING
SPECIAL-SAUCE ALL-GRISTLE DOUBLE-GRAVY
GAS EXPLODING BELLY-BLOATING LARD-ASS
BUTT BURGER...
on a sesame seed bun.

R. Piccolo

Men who wear suits gain weight only on their necks

Suits have been a male fashion staple for the last hundred years. Why? They were designed by a magician whose body was covered with copious rolls of flab. Magically, a suit can cover virtually all physical flaws.

The magician made a mistake, however. He didn't design turtleneck suits. So if you see a guy in an elegant, pinstriped suit and he has a fat neck, consider this a clue to the atrocities that lie beneath.

...AND UNDERNEATH THAT GORGEOUS ARMANI SUIT LAY THE PILLSBURY DOUGH-BOY WITH HAIR...

Men never refuse sex

It's erroneous to assume that men are sluts. They don't screw every woman who offers herself. They refuse the ones who charge too much. Men will refuse you, even when you don your crotchless panties and rubber wonder bra. I'm not talking about the guy you just met who will fuck you senseless no matter what time it is, how tired he is, or when he has to wake up in the morning. The guy who easily refuses sex is the one you've been sleeping with every night for the last million years.

MR. POTATO HEAD:
THE ULTIMATE MAN

If finding the right man was as easy as ordering dinner, you could simply ask for Mr. Combo Platter. He'd contain all of the unique attributes you want in a man. If you're not satisfied, you could always send him back or feed him to the dog.

The truth is, no one guy will ever possess every quality you're looking for. Picture the man of your dreams. Mine would be handsome, intelligent, entertaining, and loaded. He'd have a hard body, thick hair, sparkling teeth, and a reproductive organ that easily defies gravity. He'd be in touch with his feminine side. Ideally, he'd have a lot of nice furniture so I wouldn't have to redecorate if I moved in with him.

When my friends and I compare our dating experiences, we always find that for every characteristic we liked in a man, he had ten we didn't like.

I dated Tommy, who was gorgeous but boring. He was as interesting as an ancient goat chewing cud on a ninety degree afternoon. I loved staring at him, but I needed mental stimulation too. Then I found Bill, who had a brilliant sense of humor, but the sex appeal of a troll. If Bill had Tommy's looks, or Tommy had Bill's brain, I would have scored a ten. But I didn't, so I moved on to Bob, who was cute, funny *and* intelligent.

But Bob rarely showered.

Then came Freddie. He was handsome, smart, and humorous. He even knew the mechanics of personal hygiene. But he was bald. Baldness makes a man feel inferior, especially when you won't touch his head. When he had hair, women ran their fingers through it. He bitterly remembers.

Politely, I ran my hand across his scalp, pretending it didn't feel like I was stroking an iguana.

Carlos was next. He had fabulous hair. The thickest, sexiest hair I'd ever seen. Unfortunately, it didn't stop at his head. It grew rampant all over his body. He even had hair on his knuckles.

Kenny had sparkling teeth. I loved his teeth, until he showed me how he could pop them out of his mouth.

Preston had a shitload of money and a generous desire to share. But all he wanted to share was me—with his friend, Arthur.

To this day, I want only one man: Mr. Potato Head. That cute little plastic fellow whose limbs and facial features come in a separate bag is exactly what I need. How wonderful—a man I can simply assemble!

I thought of the disadvantages. I can't take a plastic guy to the opera, unless I carry him in my clutch bag. Skiing was out of the question. If I brought him into the lodge, he'd melt in front of the fireplace. But so what? He's available and if it doesn't work out, he's recyclable.

I suggested Mr. Potato Head to my friend, Donna, who looks for love in all the wrong places. She was at the police station, browsing through mug shots when I broached the subject.

"I can't be the mother of Mr. Potato Head's children!" she said. "I need something to nurture and cuddle."

Until science breathes life into Mr. Potato Head, stay optimistic.

My friend, Carolyn, the shrink, says, "Know exactly what you want and exactly what you need. Men can satisfy your wants, but don't expect them to satisfy your needs."

"What if I need a massage?" I asked.

"Don't ask him. Pay a professional. Professionals know their purpose, and they know you need a massage, not hot spicy sex."

"If my life sucks, I might need some hot spicy sex."

"If your life sucks, get yourself a better life, not a better man," she said. "Fulfill your own needs and you won't need him. If he's not needed he'll always work hard to impress you."

You can simplify things for yourself. When man hunting, make a list of everything you're looking for. Prioritize the list and eliminate anything you can replace with two pounds of imported chocolate. I'm absolutely certain you'll find Mr. Perfect, or at least Mr. Passable. But remember, searching for the ultimate man is like shopping for a used car. It's only a matter of time before the transmission goes.

DON'T LEND THIS BOOK TO YOUR FRIENDS!

(You'll never see it again!)

Get your best friend a copy...or tell her to bu¥ heR Own!

To receive a special *gift edition* autographed by the author, order by phone. Call **1-800 75 HYPER** Visa/Mastercard accepted or... Mail $9.95 ($11.95 in Canada), plus $2.00 shipping, and the adorable little coupon below.

ABOUT THE CARTOONISTS

RINA PICCOLO's cartoons have appeared in a number of magazines and newspapers including *Mademoiselle, National Lampoon, Utne Reader, The "New Breed" Newspaper,* and more. Her work has been featured in numerous cartoon anthologies including "The Best Contemporary Women's Humor" and "Women's Glibber." Her book, **Stand Back, I Think I'm Gonna Laugh**, is available through Laugh Lines Press. To order please send cheque or money order for $7.95 U.S. plus $1.00 postage to: Laugh Lines Press, P.O. Box 259, Bala Cynwyd, PA 19004. To order by phone call toll free 1-800-356-9315. Rina Piccolo lives in Toronto, Canada.

R.C. ARADIO is from Buffalo, New York, (the drinking town with the football problem.) He attended the School of Visual Arts in New York City, paid his dues, and is now preparing his forthcoming comic book, **The Targs**™, for its premier. R.C. divides his time between Buffalo, where he teaches cartooning, comic book techniques and airbrushing, and New York City.

A message to you from the author

Dear Reader,

Now that you've checked out this book, what did you think of it? Did I leave anything out? Do you have a favorite horror story that you'd like to share? I would enjoy and appreciate your feedback.

This book is the first of a series that will make the most of our favorite sport: gossip and bitching. My next book is called **The Trouble with Chocolate, Hormones, and other Addictions**. If you would like me to include your story, (an experience with a particular compulsion) write it down and dash it off. No compulsion is too goofy, no addiction too trivial. From coffee & hairspray to shoe shopping & zit picking... share your vices with all of us!

I look forward to your letters. Send 'em to:

Hypertext Books
PO Box 420686
San Diego, CA 92142

or E-mail me at HPGBooks@AOL.com

Sincerely,

Kitty

Kitty Mancini